W9-AMP-282

MY ITCHY BODY

LIZA FROMER AND FRANCINE GERSTEIN MD

Illustrated by Joe Weissmann

TUNDRA BOOKS

Published in Canada by Tundra Books, a Division of Random House of Canada Limited
One Toronto Street, Suite 300, Toronto, Ontario M5C 2V6

Published in the United States by Tundra Books of Northern New York,
P.O. Box 1030, Plattsburgh, New York 12901

Library of Congress Control Number: 2011938773

Library and Archives Canada Cataloguing in Publication

Fromer, Liza
    My itchy body / Liza Fromer and Francine Gerstein ; illustrated by Joe Weissmann.

(Body works)
ISBN 978-1-77049-311-7

    1. Skin – Juvenile literature. 2. Skin – Diseases – Juvenile literature. 3. Human body
– Juvenile literature. 4. Human physiology – Juvenile literature. I. Weissmann, Joe, 1947-
II. Gerstein, Francine III. Title. IV. Series: Body works (Toronto, Ont.)

QP88.5.F76 2012   j612.7'9   C2011-906499-5   9807

We acknowledge the financial support of the Government of Canada through the Canada
Book Fund and that of the Government of Ontario through the Ontario Media Development
Corporation's Ontario Book Initiative. We further acknowledge the support of the Canada
Council for the Arts and the Ontario Arts Council for our publishing program.

ONTARIO ARTS COUNCIL
CONSEIL DES ARTS DE L'ONTARIO

Medium: watercolor on paper

Design: Leah Springate

Printed and bound in China

1 2 3 4 5 6   17 16 15 14 13 12

Also available in this Body Works series by Liza Fromer
and Francine Gerstein MD, illustrated by Joe Weissmann

Authors' Note

The information in this book is to help you understand your body and learn why it works the way it does.

It's important that you see your family doctor at least once each year. If you're worried about your health or think you might be sick, speak to an adult and see your doctor.

Everyone knows what it feels like to be itchy. But what exactly is an itch? Generally, it's defined as an irritating feeling on your skin that makes you want to scratch. It's not a comfortable sensation. Sometimes the part of you that is itchy is covered in a rash. Other times it may look pretty normal – but it could become red and scaly if you scratch it too much.

Itchy skin (MT: pruritus) can last a few seconds or a long time. And some-times scratching an itch can make it even itchier. This is called the "scratch-itch cycle" and it can be difficult to stop.

If you get an itch, you should try to find out what's causing it so you can make it better right away. There are hundreds of causes of itches.

By the way. . .
When you see MT in this book, it stands for Medical Term.

DRY SKIN

Normal, healthy skin is covered in a thin layer of natural oil (MT: sebum), which is produced by sebaceous glands in the skin. This sebum keeps in moisture and makes your skin soft and waterproof.

Taking too many baths or swimming for long periods of time can strip the skin of its natural oils and cause dryness (MT: xeroderma). Visiting a climate where the air doesn't have a lot of moisture (humidity) in it, like the desert, can dry out your skin, too. Dry skin can also be caused by sunburn, certain medications, and medical conditions, such as diabetes mellitus. Dry skin might feel tight and uncomfortable, and it can look dull, pink, or flaky.

Dry skin is very common and can usually be treated with moisturizers. Having showers instead of baths can also help. Make sure the water isn't too hot, and stay in the shower for only a few minutes. Mild, fragrance-free soaps are best.

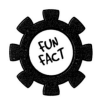 **FUN FACT** Dry skin is most common in the winter because of the dry, cold air outside and the dry, warm air inside, which comes from the furnace.

True or false?

Your skin is your body's suit of armor against bacteria. (*True*. Cracked, dry skin is more prone to infection.)

Doctor says:

"The best time to apply moisturizer is right after a bath or shower, when your skin is still a bit wet. The moisturizer will help your body absorb the water on your skin."

SKIN INFLAMMATION

Skin inflammation (MT: dermatitis) is your body's way of responding to things that bother it – like infection, injury, or irritation. Even though it may not sound like it, inflammation is your body's way of trying to protect itself. The classic signs of skin inflammation are redness, swelling, warmth, and pain.

There are different types of dermatitis. Two common types are contact dermatitis (caused by substances that "contact," or touch, your skin) and atopic dermatitis (otherwise known as eczema).

CONTACT DERMATITIS

There are two types of contact dermatitis: allergic and irritant. Both types can cause itchiness, redness, dryness, scaling, swelling, and blistering.

ALLERGIC CONTACT DERMATITIS

Allergic dermatitis is caused by a person's sensitivity to something that touches the skin. Poison ivy, nickel in some jewelry, and fragrances in some lotions can cause these reactions in some people.

Urushiol is an oil that is found in poison ivy, poison oak, and poison sumac plants. About 50 percent of the population is allergic to this

oil. When these people come in contact with one of these plants (or even with something that has touched one of these plants, like a dog), they develop allergic dermatitis. Sometimes it takes a few exposures to develop the dermatitis. The rash usually occurs from a few hours to two days after exposure to the plant. It looks red, has blisters in a line or circle pattern, and lasts around two weeks . . . yuck!

Poison ivy, oak, and sumac all grow in North America. Poison ivy and poison oak each have three leaves on each stem. Remember: "Leaves in three, let it be!" This rule doesn't apply to poison sumac, which has many leaves per stem.

To avoid touching these plants while walking through the woods, wear long pants, socks, and shoes. If you touch one of them by chance, immediately wash the affected area for five minutes with soap and water. If you do not wash it, the oil will be absorbed into your skin after about an hour.

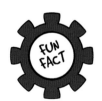 **FUN FACT** Urushiol oil can remain on clothing and shoes for years. Use soap and water to wash clothes and shoes that have been in contact with these plants — or you could get contact dermatitis from your clothes and shoes!

IRRITANT CONTACT DERMATITIS

Irritant contact dermatitis is caused when irritants like harsh soaps or detergents damage the skin faster than the skin can repair itself. Irritants remove the skin's natural oils and moisture, which allows the irritants to penetrate more deeply. This can cause more damage by triggering inflammation.

You can get irritant dermatitis from a single exposure to an irritant (like a strong chemical) or from repeated exposure to milder irritants (like soap and water). Washing your hands is a good thing to do because it washes away dirt and infectious particles (like cold viruses), but too much hand-washing – even just with water – can be very irritating to the skin.

The hands are a common area for irritant dermatitis because we use our hands to touch a lot of things. People with jobs in cleaning, hospital care, hairdressing, and food preparation are more likely to get irritant dermatitis because they work with irritants such as soaps and detergents.

The best way to avoid getting irritant dermatitis is to avoid the irritant! But if you do get irritant dermatitis, a medicated cream from your doctor or a moisturizer might help.

FUN FACTS

#1 People with dry skin or eczema experience more contact dermatitis – likely because their skin barrier has already been compromised.

#2 Some people can get a rash underneath their ring if soap and water get trapped there.

True or False?

Using a pen or pencil to do a lot of homework can cause homework dermatitis of the first three fingers. (*False*. But good try!)

ATOPIC DERMATITIS

Atopic dermatitis (eczema) is a skin condition that can cause itchy, dry, and inflamed skin on and off for a long time. It is common in childhood, affecting up to 20 percent of kids. Many outgrow eczema by the time they are adults.

We don't really know why eczema happens. One theory might be that the skin doesn't function normally, allowing moisture to escape and irritants to enter.

Sometimes things in the environment can make eczema worse. Examples of these triggers might be certain soaps, perfumes, and things that some people are allergic to. Dry skin can also make eczema worse. Moisturizers can help to improve dryness. Many people with eczema also use medicated creams from the doctor.

#1 Eczema occurs most frequently on the face, inside the elbows, behind the knees, and on the hands and feet.

#2 With eczema, sometimes the skin gets worse (flare-ups) and sometimes it improves or clears up (remissions).

True or False?

You can't spread eczema to other people because it is not contagious. (*True.*)

Doctor says:

"Eczema runs in families (is genetic) and is associated with asthma and allergies in the environment (like hay fever)."

HIVES

Hives (MT: urticaria) are red, itchy, raised areas of skin. They can be different shapes, like round or ring-like, and they can be as small as one-tenth of an inch (just a few millimeters) and as big as a few inches (more than five centimeters). Individual hives can even join together to create a patch or map-like pattern. Although some last just a few minutes, each hive usually lasts a few hours and is then replaced by a new one. Hives can even change shape. Some people call hives welts or wheals. Approximately 10 percent of all people develop hives at some point in their lives.

There are many causes of hives, including allergic reactions to medications, food, and insect stings. Viruses and some illnesses cause hives. However, we usually can't figure out the exact cause. Talk about frustrating . . .

Occasionally, hives can occur with a dangerous swelling in your throat and airways, making it hard to breathe. This is a medical emergency!

Sometimes hives go away on their own, but other times you need to take medicine or have an injection.

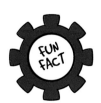 **Some people even get hives from the sun or from exercising.**

True or False?
You can have only one hive on your body or you can have dozens. (*True.*)

Doctor says:
"Hives are classified as acute (lasting less than six weeks) or chronic (lasting more than six weeks)."

BITES AND INFESTATIONS

If you've ever been bitten by a mosquito, you know about itchy bug bites. Mosquito bites usually cause red itchy bumps. Just thinking about them can make you itchy!

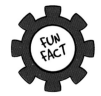

Only female mosquitoes bite (feed on the blood of humans and animals). Male mosquitoes feed on flower nectar.

A louse is also a bug, but it is much smaller than a mosquito. There are different types of lice. The one that people hear the most about is head lice. Head lice spreads easily when people are in close contact. That's why it's common among children in school and daycare. Lice can't fly, but they can crawl super fast. They are transmitted by hair-to-hair (head-to-head) contact or by sharing brushes, combs, or hats. The most common symptom of head lice is an itchy scalp.

Lice lay eggs, called nits, on strands of hair near the scalp. Nits are very small (as small as a grain of salt), teardrop-shaped, and whitish-gray in color. Luckily there are special shampoos you can use to get rid of lice and nits.

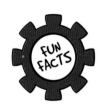

#1 The kind of lice that live on people do not live on their pets.

#2 It is possible to have lice without being itchy.

True or False?

If someone has lice, it means that they aren't clean enough. (*False.* Lice also like clean hair.)

INFECTIONS

Chicken pox is caused by a virus called varicella zoster virus (VZV), and it is very itchy and contagious. The rash usually starts on the face and trunk and spreads to the arms and legs. At first it may look like little red bumps, but the bumps quickly turn into small blisters. Chicken pox is transmitted when a person with the virus breathes, coughs, or sneezes, and someone nearby breathes it in. You can also catch chicken pox by touching the blisters of someone who is infected.

A person is contagious with chicken pox a few days before the rash starts and until all of the blisters have crusted over. While some people may get only a few blisters, others can have hundreds – talk about itchy! Children with chicken pox may also have a fever, feel unwell, and have a decreased appetite. Usually chicken pox is worse in adults than in children. Treatment is often given to help the fever and the itch, although sometimes special antiviral medications are needed.

Ringworm (MT: tinea) is another itchy skin infection. It is caused by an organism called a fungus (it's not a worm). The name ringworm refers to the typical ring shape of the rash. A fungus is an infectious organism that is bigger than a virus or bacteria. The ringworm rash typically looks round and red, with a scaly border. It can affect the scalp, body, feet, and nails.

People can get ringworm by skin-to-skin contact with an infected person, or even a pet. Ringworm can also be transmitted by contact with objects that an infected person or pet has touched, such as a shower stall, gym mat, comb, or brush.

Ringworm is usually treated with antifungal creams or medicines. To avoid spreading ringworm, you should make sure to finish the entire treatment the doctor has prescribed, minimize close contact with your friends, and avoid sharing personal things like hats, towels, and clothes until the rash has healed.

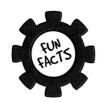

FUN FACTS

#1 Ever since a chicken pox vaccine was introduced in the 1990s, there have been fewer cases of the virus.

#2 Chicken pox rash usually develops between 10 to 21 days after contact with an infected person.

True or False?

Ringworm of the foot is referred to as athlete's foot. (*True*. And you don't have to be an athlete to get it.)

INTERNAL ILLNESSES

Some illnesses inside the body, like problems with your liver or kidney, can also cause itchy skin. This itchy skin can have rashes or look normal, and it usually affects the person's entire body instead of just one small part.

STRESS

Even though it may sound strange, feeling nervous or stressed can cause you to feel itchy. Stress can also aggravate skin that's already itchy. It's even possible to feel itchy just by thinking about something that's itchy (like lice or mosquitoes).

Isn't it amazing what your itchy body can do!

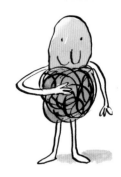

Glossary

Asthma: A disease of the respiratory system that causes the airways to narrow, leading to wheezing, coughing, and shortness of breath.

Bacteria: Microscopic organisms that cause disease or infection.

Contagious: Capable of being transmitted from one person to another.

Diabetes mellitus: People who have this disease, sometimes called sugar diabetes, have a high level of sugar in their blood.

Fungi: Organisms that are larger than viruses and bacteria. Some are microscopic and some can be seen by the naked eye.

Hay fever: There is no "fever" in hay fever. Symptoms like sneezing, runny nose, nasal congestion, and itchy eyes and throat are caused by an allergy to particles in the environment.

Humidity: The amount of water in the air.

Microorganism: A super-small living thing, like a bacteria, that our eyes can't see. Some are helpful and some are harmful.

Rash: A rash may cause the skin to change color or have dots, blotches, bumps, or blisters. It can also make skin feel itchy, warm, dry, or painful.

Virus: A microscopic infectious agent that can only reproduce in a living cell.